O9-BTL-906

HURON COUNTY LIBRARY

3 6492 0037075 8

782.420268 Bow

The illustrated Canadian
songbook.

(CDN) L

PRICE: $24.95 (3559/se)

We dedicate this book to the memory of

Bill Merrill of CFCF television, Montreal.

He was taken away far too soon.

But at least we had the chance to make him laugh.

Welcome to the world's biggest album sleeve!

We hope you enjoy the cartoons.
However, if you don't,
we had nothing to do with choosing them.

There may be minor discrepancies between
the printed lyrics and the songs as performed live.
This is normal.
Do not adjust your brain.

Published in Canada in 2003
By McArthur & Company
322 King St. West, Suite 402
Toronto, Ontario
M5V 1J2
www.mcarthur-co.com

Cartoons Copyright © 2003 Terry Mosher
Text Copyright © 2003 Bowser & Blue

The use of any part of this publication reproduced, transmitted in any form or by any means,
electronic, mechanical, photocopying, recording or otherwise stored in a retrieval system,
without the expressed written consent of the publisher, is an infringement of the copyright law.

National Library of Canada Cataloguing in Publication

Bowser & Blue (Musical duo)
The illustrated Canadian songbook / by Bowser & Blue ; illustrated by Aislin.

Accompanied by a CD.
ISBN 1-55278-379-0

1. Humorous songs—Texts. I. Aislin II. Title.

ML54.6.B788 2003   782.42164'0268   C2003-904013-5

Cover illustration by AISLIN; cover photo by George Belinsky
Layout, Design and Electronic Imaging by Mary Hughson-Mosher
Printed and Bound in Canada by Transcontinental Printing, Inc.

The publisher would like to acknowledge the financial support of the Government of Canada through the
Book Publishing Industry Development Program, the Canada Council, and the Ontario Arts Council for our
publishing activities. We also acknowledge the Government of Ontario through the Ontario Media
Development Corporation Ontario Book Initiative.

10 9 8 7 6 5 4 3 2 1

The Illustrated Canadian Songbook
by BOWSER & BLUE

With cartoons by

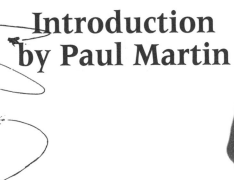

Introduction
by Paul Martin

McArthur & Company

Toronto

Table of Contents

Introduction

When one thinks of Canada, a whole litany of proud and noteworthy things comes to mind. The Rocky Mountains. Portage and Main. The Liberal Party. Wayne Gretzky. Frozen tundra. The Liberal Party. Parliament Hill. Poutine. Peggy's Cove. The Liberal Party.

And then there's Wayne & Shuster. And then there's that guy Bob at Juste Pour Rire. And Carole at the coffee shop in Ville Émard. Now she's funny. And then there's Bowser and Blue.

For 25 years, Bowser and Blue have brought their "unique" brand of humour to the stage, poking fun at Canadian – especially Québecois – personalities and institutions that we very often take far too seriously. In particular, their sharp and satiric look at politics can only be described as thought-provoking and hilarious. Except when it's about me.

To appreciate how good they are, you only had to attend the annual "Hilarity for Charity" fund-raising comedy event in Ottawa a couple of years ago. If that had been a competition to find the best international comedy troupe, Bowser and Blue would have won hands down. Not only can they outwit the best of them, but they can actually sing as well!

Coming from Quebec, I can tell you that Bowser and Blue are as much of an institution there as traffic jams on the Champlain Bridge. This book is proof that few know Quebec better than they.

Add in the exceptional cartooning talent of Aislin and you've got a real winner in *The Illustrated Canadian Songbook* by Bowser and Blue. I couldn't be more thrilled that this truly special artist has lent his huge talent to the project.

Anyone looking to share in the lighter side of Canadian and Quebec life would be wise to pick up this book. It's worth every chuckle.

Hon. Paul Martin
Member of Parliament
LaSalle-Émard

We're All Here

We came here to work and to play
We came a hundred years ago
We came yesterday

We came to a brand new nation
We came through customs
And immigration

We came from England and France
We crossed the Bering Strait
Without any pants

To a land where the wild geese honk
We came here to build
We came here to bonk

We came from Asia and Spain
We came here from Africa
We came from Ukraine

Went out one night for a beer
Got drunk, fell down
And woke up here

We came by sea and by air
We came anyhow
We came from everywhere

With our feet we did vote
And now we're all
In the same rusty boat

We're all here
With the moose
And the bear

We're all here
In our long underwear

We're all here
And what do we share?
We're all here –
Because we're not all there

Canada Day

Rick: *It rained on our Canada Day parade. But rain is very Canadian. It teaches us what it is like to live in Vancouver.*

George: *Paul Martin made a speech. He said he'd eliminated the federal deficit. He put it in his wife's name.*

Rick: *At the end of the parade we were reminded that once again Canada was voted best country in the world by the United Nations. Could that be because so many of them have relatives now living here?*

George: *I like playing in Canada. People are so friendly. In fact they are user-friendly. I know, because they said to us: "Youse 'r friendly."*

In The Key Of "Eh?"

After saying something
Americans say: "Huh?"
And if you go to France you'll hear
Them say: "N'est-ce pas?"
Teenagers, OK? Make a statement, OK?
And then they go: "OK?"
But in Canada every thought
Is followed with an: "Eh?"

This "A" we utter
Where does it come from?
It isn't "A" as in vitamin
Or "A" as in "Atom bomb"
It doesn't indicate the grade
For which students sweat
In fact it has nothing to do
With the alphabet

It separates the "We"
From the "They"
From Vancouver to St. John's
To Hudson Bay
You can drink a Coke
Or drive a Chevrolet
But you're Canadian if you say
"Eh?"

It's a verbal indiscretion
An involuntary yelp
It's more than just an "Eh"
It's a cry for help
We always add "Eh?" when
We have a point to make
To check that you're still listening
Or, indeed, are still awake

Why do we always put an "Eh"
At the end of everything we say?
It's a law we all seem to obey
And when we do it
We give ourselves away
Eh?

CANADIAN A.A. MEETING

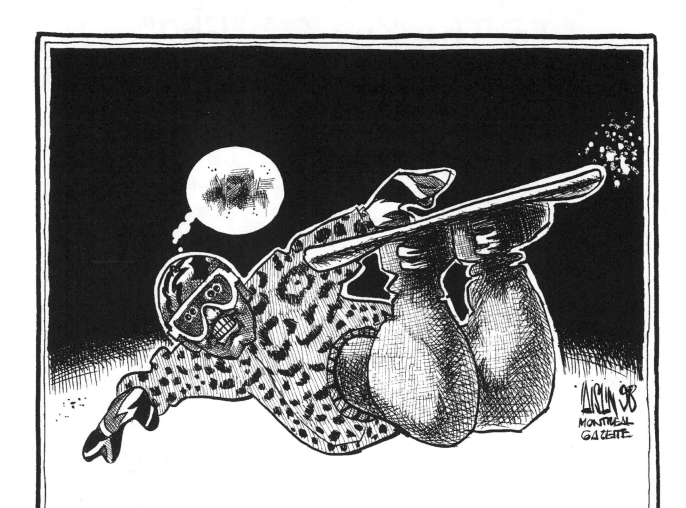

ON THE OTHER HAND, WHO AMONGST US WOULD EVEN ATTEMPT THIS SORT OF THING WITHOUT FIRST GETTING AS STONED AS POSSIBLE ON WHATEVER SUBSTANCE WAS HANDILY AVAILABLE?

Rick: *I like playing in B.C. There is all that smoked salmon.*

George: *They'll smoke anything in B.C.*

The Canadian Psychedelic Snowboarding Team

At the Winter Olympics
Wild and free
The mountains were high
And so were we
We don't remember
We don't really care
If you can remember the Olympics
You weren't really there

Because when they told
Us to go for the gold
We thought it meant, like, something
That could be rolled

The Canadian psychedelic
Snowboarding team

It's a difficult skill
That we've honed
We should get a medal
Just for doing it stoned
The Spice Girls have been making
A lot of noise
But are you ready for
"The Herbal Boys"?

I tested positively
But I can't help it you see
You get that way just from living
In B.C.

The Canadian psychedelic
Snowboarding team

Rick: *What is a Canadian? You know you're Canadian when you set aside one day a year to silicone your mukluks.*

George: *You know you're Canadian when you're 45 years old and you still play hockey to win.*

Rick: *You know you're Canadian when the national team wins a bronze medal – and you're excited.*

George: *You know you're Canadian when the government is suggesting there should be a $5 charge to see the doctor, and you're outraged.*

Rick: *You know you're Canadian when you look at American money and say: "They're all the same colour, how do they know which is which?"*

George: *You know you're Canadian when they play your national anthem and you don't know the words.*

Rick: *You know you're Canadian when you've "written your name in the snow."*

Writing My Name In The Snow

Writing my name in the snow-ho
Writing my name in the snow-ho
I'm Canadian so-ho
I'm writing my name in the snow-ho-ho
Ho! Ho! Ho!

I like a challenge so I try
To cross my tees and dot my I's
Yes, I can go from A to Zee
But, candidly
It's the closest I get to poetry
The closest I get to poetry
When I'm
Writing my name in the snow-ho

Writing my name in the snow-ho
Whenever I've gotta go-ho

I'm writing my name in the snow-ho-ho
Ho! Ho! Ho!

Jesus changed the water from the well
Into wine and that was swell
But no one calls it a miracle when
I change the wine
Back into water again
Back to water again
When I'm
Writing my name in the snow-ho

Writing my name in the snow-ho
I'm Canadian so
I'm writing my name in the snow-ho-ho
Ho! Ho! Ho!

George: *Canada is a wonderful country. It's where the Fathers of Confederation got together with the Mothers of Invention, and created the Kids in the Hall.*

Canadian Culture

Does anybody share?
Canadian culture
Does anybody care?
Canadian culture

You can spot a Canadian
It's easy as pie
A Canadian won't say soldier
He'll say: "Army guy"

Canada's like vichyssoise
Have you heard this slur?
Because it's cold, it's part French
And it's difficult to stir

You'll see it every day
Canadian culture
Go shopping at the Bay
Canadian culture

We've been searching everywhere
Searching here, searching there
Searching for Canadian culture

Is it in a BeaverTail?
Is it a beluga whale?
Is it in an Eskimo sculpture?

Is it in a Lightfoot tune?
In the cry of a loon?
A can of maple syrup on the table?

Is it in the Bay of Fundy?
Is it shopping on a Sunday?
Is it Anne of frigging Green Gables?

Will Canada survive?
Some folks are quite leery
I mean, it works in practice
But it just doesn't work in theory

Looking all around
Canadian culture
Something going down
Canadian culture

I Want That Stick

I've always been a hockey fan
Collected tons of things
Original six logos
And Stanley cup rings
I've got some real prize items
And some that make me laugh
Like a Guy Lafleur helmet
(That's impossible)
And Eddie Shack's autograph
(That's impossible too)

But now all I want
Is the ultimate souvenir
I want the stick that McSorley used
To clobber Don Brashear

I want that stick
I really want that stick
If I could get a hold of it
Now that would be a trick
Maybe it sounds weird to you
Maybe it's just sick
But I really, really want that stick!

I've spoken to the Canucks
And I've spoken to the Bruins
It's no use to McSorley now
His career's in ruins
I had a word with the linesmen

And a chat with the ref
I would have spoken to Brashear
But apparently he'd gone deaf
Somebody ran off with it
That's absolutely clear
I mean the stick that McSorley used
To clobber Don Brashear

I want that stick
I really want that stick
He's probably holding onto it himself
The rotten prick
Maybe it sounds weird to you
Or maybe it's just sick
But I really, really want that stick!

Some want the impossible
And I say lots of luck
Like a Gordie Howe elbow pad
Or that Henderson puck
But it's amazing what they'll give you
If you just say "please"
A friend of mine says he has
One of Bobby Orr's knees

Some want almost anything
That's signed by '99'
But I'm looking for the hockey stick
That Gretzky didn't sign

I want that stick
I really want that stick
It's worth a fortune now
I've done the arithmetic
It would look great next to
My bit of Holyfield's ear
I want the stick that McSorley used
To clobber Don Brashear

Now, there's a rumour going round
And I don't know if it's true
They say that Don Brashear
Is keeping an eye out for it, too

If he finds it he'll treasure it
He's got a lot of class

'Till he meets McSorley and
He can tell him to shove it
– Under glass
(I know what you were thinking,
But that would decrease its value –
To another collector)

I want that stick
I really want that stick
I've spent hours on the Internet
Going point and bloody click
Maybe it sounds weird to you
And maybe it's just sick
But I really, really want that stick

Welcome To Darkest Canada

The great Canadian adventure
Is out in the open air
Trekking across the tundra
With a coureur de bois named Pierre
It's the Canada we sell to the tourists
Sometimes we fall for it too
Suckered by pictures of glaciers
And Trudeau in his frigging canoe

Welcome to darkest Canada
Welcome to darkest Canada
A continent of mystery
Barely touched by history
Feel the terror and the fear
As you disappear
In darkest Canada

Trekking across the tundra
You'll probably say a prayer
You don't get eaten alive by mosquitoes
Or disembowelled by a grizzly bear
Sitting around the campfire
Scraping the shit off your shoe
You're wondering what's for dinner
You have a horrible feeling it's – you

Welcome to darkest Canada
Welcome to darkest Canada
Miles and miles of trees and bears
Black flies swarming in the air
One question comes up clear
"What am I doin' here?"
In darkest Canada

AISLIN 81
THE MONTREAL
GAZETTE

Rick: *Every night of the week roadhouses and sports bars across Canada offer a different activity to encourage the creation and filling of beer bellies.*

George: *Hey, don't call this a beer belly.*
It's a portable, expandable, liquid malt storage unit.

Tuesday Night Is "Wing Night"

When Canadians seek culture
Of which they can partake
Do they flock to Stratford?
Or Niagara-on-the-Lake?
That's OK I guess
For the privileged few
But as for average Canadians
I'll tell you what they do

Tuesday night is "Wing Night"
And it's hard to get a seat
For that part of the chicken
That no one used to eat

Wednesday night is "Ladies Night"
Girls drink free till ten
They keep the guys penned up
Behind a rope till then

Thursday's "Karaoke Night"
It's high technology
You'll hear drunken customers
Sing "My Way" way off key

Friday is "Lambada Night"
Which I do endorse
Some call it dance, I call it
Sexual intercourse

Saturday's "Wet-T-Shirt Night"
For bodies young and pert
If you win first prize you get
A dry T-shirt

Sunday night is "Bungee Night"
A bouncer's nightmare
Because on bungee night
There's bouncers everywhere

Monday is a special night
It's the night they call
"Dwarf Tossing, Giant Screen
 Tractor Pulling, Mud Wrestling

Chippendale, Yuk Yuks
Velcro diving
Two-For-One
Bumdarts Night!

Let's Play Bum Darts

You don't have to be a Prof
Or a Master of Arts
Anyone is smart enough
To play the game of Bum Darts

Grip a quarter with your butt
This is how the fun starts
Then you drop it in a cup
Now you're playing Bum Darts

Careful on your first approach
Pay attention to the coach
Clench the coin tightly
In your crease
Till you feel the time is right
Hold on to that quarter tight
Soon will come
The moment of release

Bum Darts is catching on
From Vancouver to Saint John
It's a language that everybody speaks
Any time, or any place,
It's got style. It's got grace
And with Bum Darts
You'll have firmer cheeks

29

Rick: *In 1991, Gwen Jacobs, a student at the University of Guelph, challenged a law that gave men the right to take their shirts off in public but not women. She won her case.*
George: *Thus giving rise to the slogan: "Ontario, Yours To Uncover."*

Why Are We Busting The Breast?

One very hot day in the summer that year
A woman was walking through Guelph
She saw bare-chested men enjoying the sun
And said: "I think I'll do that myself."
So she paused in her stroll to take off her top
And then, much to her disgust
A passing policeman told her to stop
And said: "Young woman, this is a bust!"

Why are we busting the breast?
This question must be addressed
Why make an issue
Of mammary tissue?
Why are we busting the breast?

Then hundreds of women
All took up her cause
They heard she was going to court
They said: "This is a fight for topless rights
And she's going to need our support!"
They marched in protest

All baring their breasts
And saying: "The law is an ass."
Enduring the cries of hundreds of guys
Who descended with cameras en masse

Saying why are we busting the breast?
This question must be addressed
Why make an issue
Of mammary tissue?
Why are we busting the breast?

The judge concerned
Said: "What must be learned
And what this court must decide
Is how much of the body
No matter which gender,
Society requires us to hide
This may seem frivolous at first sight
But in fact it's a serious charge
Because men also have breasts
And some of them are quite large

Why are we busting the breast?
This simply must be addressed
Why make an issue
Of mammary tissue?
Why are we busting the breast?

Then the judge handed down a ruling
And this is what she said:
"It's the law, not the breast
That must be redressed
Which led to this woman's wrongful arrest
Which started her off on her legal quest
To prove that she had been oppressed
By a law which simply had not progressed
Because it's no crime to bare your breast!"

Why are we busting the breast?
As a mammal I don't understand
If there's a part of the body
That does only good
It's the mammary gland!

We often compare ourselves with the U.S.
And often they come out the best
But they only have the right to bear arms
And we have the right to bare breasts

I'm glad they weren't convicted
That would have been a bummer
I'm glad that justice triumphed
And I'm glad every summer

We're no longer busting the breast
I'm glad we got that off our chest
Why make an issue
Of mammary tissue
We're no longer busting the breast!

Club Soda Anecdote

Rick: *We used to do an instrumental dance number called "The Dance of the Two Soli-Dudes," wearing tutus and tiaras. We performed this for the last time at the new Club Soda, on St. Laurent just below St. Catherine Street. It's quite a funky neighbourhood. Full of panhandlers and rubies and scary-looking hookers. Just before the show, the stage manager took us, in costume, outside the back door to enter the stage from another outside door. But that door was locked. She told us to wait and then disappeared, leaving us standing on a side street in the red light district, one in a Canada tutu and the other in a Quebec tutu. We were locked out and felt very vulnerable and conspicuous. But nobody even noticed us.*

George: *Small businesses are doing well in Canada.*
Of course, some of them started out as big businesses.

Heartbreak Nortel

Since my money left me
I've found a new place to dwell
On the corner of lowly street
At Heartbreak Nortel
And we feel low

Nortel has exploded
The TSE balloon
There's a whole lot of Canadians now
Who won't be retiring soon
And we feel low

Heartbreak Nortel
Heartbreak – If you didn't sell

I didn't sell at sixty
At fifty I didn't stir
I waited till it hit two bucks
Duh!

We were talking fibre optics
And high-tech instruments
Now we're talking savings banks
And two-and-a-half percent
And we feel low

They haven't gone out of business
That stock will rise again
It'll go back to a hundred bucks
But we'll all be dead by then

Heartbreak Nortel
Heartbreak – If you didn't sell

Rick: Canada is a wonderful country. It's the only place in the world where they take Canadian money at par!

George: The loony is flying a little higher since this song was written. But who knew? Economists are only there to make weather forecasters look good.

The Loony Is Down

The loony, the loony
The loony is down
It keeps going down
And it won't turn around

The loony, the loony
It's just a lame duck
Our poor little dollar
Is not worth a
Buck

When surveys of all
The world's countries are done
Canada frequently rates number one
Are we the best country?
We'll never know
There's nowhere else
We can afford to go

The loony, the loony
The loony is low
The Prime Minister says
"It's no problem," though
Here's my message to Mr. Chrétien
Thanks a million
Canadian

Rick: *I collect Canadian coins.*
You never know, one day they might be worth something.

The Old Ten Dollar Bill

Everything you want to know about Canada
Is written on this ten dollar bill

The bill is coloured purple
Which rhymes with maple surple
That well-known product of our nation
Made of paper from a tree
From our lumber industry
And it's wrinkled
Like half the population

The number ten is there
Because Canada is where
We have provinces
And they number ten
And the translator's tricks
Have turned the ten to "dix"
Because our founding fathers
Were all men

There's a picture of Sir John
A man with lots of talent
But they had to write his name

So nobody would claim
Hey – isn't that Woody Allen?

A coat of arms is on the note
Because to live here you need a coat
You never know when
There'll be a snow flurry
And the motto's latin words
Remind us of snowbirds
"Anne Murray usque Anne Murray"

The lion's (lyin's) in recognition
Of our politicians
And the unicorn is for the Irish Rovers
In spite of what they're called
They're not Irish at all
They're Canadians and live in Vancouver

The bill it has two sides
Just like our government
The word Canada is inked
Although it's not distinct
Probably so as not to give offence

On the back there is a scene
You might ask –
"What does it mean?"
It can't just be there by mistake
It's a representation
Of our shaky federation
It's a picture of Meech friggin' lake

A bird has got its wish
It has caught a fish
What kind matters not one iota
We all understand
Especially those in Newfoundland
That the bird has exceeded its quota

Our head of state's the queen
But her picture is not there
Although she's head of state
She must think we're second-rate
She's got so much on her plate
She lives elsewhere

Everything you want to know about Canada
Is right here on this ten dollar bill
And I keep it and I always will
I never leave it on the window sill
So when I'm being questioned
Or I'm being grilled
I just show them my old ten dollar bill

A Scrum With M. Chrétien

Q: Mister Chrétien, Mister Chrétien!
What do you intend to do about the loony?

Chrétien: *Mel Lastman will have to look after himself!*

Q: Mister Chrétien, was Paul Martin fired, or did he quit?

Chrétien: *Yes.*

Q: But you had a special relationship with Mr. Martin?

Chrétien: *Yes, we worked well together. He does not say what he is knowing, and I don't know what I'm saying.*

Q: Sir, what will you do when you retire?

Chrétien: *I will spend more time with my family. That is what I want. It's not what they want, but it's what I want.*

Q: Are you going to pick a successor?

Chrétien: *I told the Canadian people, I will do my job. I have a job to do, and it's my job to do my job until I don't have my job, that's my job. Then, it will be someone else's job to do my job. But it's not my job to pick the guy who will do my job.*

Q: Will you stay in Shawinigan?

Chrétien: *Yes. You know, the people of Saint-Maurice, we are a close-knitting community. We have no village idiot. So, we all have to take turns.*

Q: Mister Chrétien, when you hosted the summit of the Americas you met President Bush. How did that go?

Chrétien: *He was happy. I don't think I have seen an American President so happy since I told President Clinton we were going to Beaver Lake.*

Q: They say Mr. Bush doesn't know much about Canada.

Chrétien: *That's true. He thought that the Plains of Abraham was an airline.*

Q: Sir, you sent Canada's troops to a bleak, inhospitable, rugged, uncivilized place.

Chrétien: *They went to Sudbury?*

Q: Afghanistan, sir. And what exactly are the troops going to do?

Chrétien: *They will do their job. And the job of the Canadian soldier is to obey questions without orders.*

Q: Back to domestic issues, sir.
What went wrong with the gun registry?

Chrétien: *Well, who knew that Canadians would have so many guns? They don't need to have guns. The Army has no guns.*

Q: Sir, why do you think the Canadian Alliance dumped Stockwell Day?

Chrétien: *He was too far to the right.*

Q: Too far to the right?

Chrétien: *Yes. And when he wore that wet suit you could see that. That's why he could not control his caucus. I control my caucus, and I have a big caucus.*

Rick: The subject of Canadian Culture came up recently in Parliament during question period. You'll notice they don't call it answer period. Ottawa is known to Canadians as the Bay of Funding. If you live in Ottawa, is that capital punishment? They say everyone gets the

government they deserve, so what did we do?
Ladies & gentlemen, senator Dustballs.

We Are The Old Farts

When every bone seems to audibly groan
As you rise from a sitting position
And the numbers you keep
In your little black book
Are not girlfriends – they're all physicians
You're deeply suspicious of cellular phones
You feel they're a new form of voodoo
When you go to a funeral
The guy in the casket
Seems to look better than you do
When anything new is suspicious to you
And whatever it is, you're agin' it
These are exactly the qualifications
You need for a job in the senate

We are Canada's senators
We have made our mark
Here there are more dinosaurs
Than in Jurassic Park

We're the old farts, the old farts
We drool and we doze
We were all born in the year of
Our lord... only knows
We're ready to fight till our last breath

We'll vanquish our enemies
We'll bore them to death
Too old to be swayed
Too rich to be bought
We're the House of Sober Second Thought

We've been here since time immemorial
We've seen every government trick
We're experienced in matters senatorial
When we were young
The Dead Sea was only sick

We're the old farts, the old farts
We wear the old school tie
Sometimes I still chase women
But I can't remember why
Hear us all talk at once
Hear our dentures clack
We can't get the push
We can't get the sack
We can't tell an orgasm
From a heart attack
Too old to be swayed
Too rich to be bought
We're the House of Sober Second Thought

The Curling Song

Curling is good fun
(So leave the pub)
And this is how it's done
(And join a club)
There's nothing that's at all
Unorthodox

Sliding down the ice
(Four mates or spouses)
It can be so nice
(Aim for two houses)
Be careful with the hand
That cradles the rocks

The stone slows to a creep
It's time for you to sweep
You didn't calculate
The right amount of weight
To hurl

Gradually you learn
How to make it turn
Or rather, as they say
To make it
Curl

When it comes to winter sport
(When it is cold)
It is generally thought
(So we are told)
That hockey is the game
To which
We flock

But if you actually play
(Participate)
Then curling wins the day
(It's really great)
In Canada more people curl
Than hock

And the hero who can curl
Always gets the girl
She tells the friends she phones
That he plays with "The Stones"

And she will be his bride
Together they will slide
He will naturally sweep
Her off
Her feet

Rick: *We dedicate this song to Rob Roy, the Scottish Robin Hood, who took from the rich – and kept it.*

'Twas The Scots That Built This Country!

'Twas the Scots that built this country
It should never be forgot
In each Canadian family
Somewhere there's a Scot

When Sir John A. Macdonald
Looked out across this land
What he saw before him
A Scot would understand

Those first few encounters
With the savages were hot
(It's "Indians," not "Savages")
I'm referring to the Scots!

St. Andrew's ball is lavish
In towns both great and small
All around the world the Scots
Are famous for their balls

Wherever Scotsmen travelled
There were two things
That they brought
Whisky (and containers)
The containers were the Scots!

'Twas the Scots that built this country
By the Scots this land was built
Not by pea soup or Yorkshire pudding
But by porridge, pipe, and kilt

While politicians argue
What is right and what is not
They do it in the comfort
Of buildings made by Scots

In every corporation
They've always saved a spot
For a portrait of their founder
A penny-pinching
Glowering red-faced
Whisky-drinking
Presbyterian, Anhedonic
Bagpipe-squeezing
Caber-tossing
Apoplectic, Haggis-eating Scot!

'Twas the Scots that built this country
With great big hairy knees
We owe a debt of gratitude
Two more whiskys, please!

When I Was A Federal Bureaucrat

Sung by Jacques Parizeau

When I was a federal bureaucrat
I once took a train to Medicine Hat
Looked out the window
And it struck me that
French did not exist

So there I sat in the railway car
And I realized how different we are
And by the time I got to Banff, ah ha!
I was a separatist

So there I was, a different man
And I knew right then
I would need a plan
I categorized all my demands
And I made a list

I polished my plan so carefully
That now I can be leader
Of my own country!
(He polished his plan so carefully
That now he can be leader
of his own country)

I knew when I wrote it
That years would go by
The Canadian people
Would never comply
I am impossible to satisfy
I am a separatist

Those federalists they can't scare me
When they argue economically
I've got a degree from the L.S.E.
(The London School of Economics,
madam)
I am a pragmatist

Since the Plains of Abraham
I claim that Canada is a sham
And I'll go on and on ad nauseam
I am a separatist

I polished my plan so carefully
That now I can be leader
Of my own country!
(He polished his plan so carefully
That now he can be leader
Of his own country)

THE THING THAT JUST WON'T GO AWAY!

And now that it's so close at hand
It's all turned out the way I planned
It's funny how it all began
With a train ride out west
(In the bar car)

And when we finally see that day
For which I fervently hope and pray

It'll finally be your turn to say
"I am a separatist!"
I polished my plan so carefully
Everyone will soon be singing
"Mon Pays"
(He polished his plan so carefully
Everyone will soon be singing
"Mon Pays")

51

Rick: *The English and the French should learn how to communicate with each other. It's as if we spoke two completely different languages!*

George: *Rick's bilingual. He speaks French twice a year.*

Louise, Louise

I was watching TV
One night in my home
In my cosy Westmount encampment
When I saw a young woman
Whose name was Louise
Complaining that English was rampant

Rampant? I thought
What on earth does she mean?
My thesaurus says
"Excessive, and rank
Unbridled, and wanton
Luxuriant and raging"
I'm a bad boy – I should be spanked

I wrote her a letter and said
"We must meet"
Even though we've had no introduction
I'm ready to throw myself
Down at your feet
If you'll give me some
Private instruction

"Louise," I wrote,
"Please meet me tonight."
She replied: "Never, hostie!"
I was excited but just to be sure
I said: "Never?
Or neuf heures et demie?"

Louise, Louise
I'm down on my knees
I've been bad and now I'm confessin'
I'm loose and immoral
I've failed my French oral
Please won't you teach me a lesson

She came through my French windows
Dressed as a French maid
With French bread, French wine
And a kiss
We locked her French poodle
Outside and I said
"It just doesn't get
Any Frencher than this!"

53

Though she was attractive
And très charmante
In some ways her behaviour was strange
She insisted on putting a sign
On the doorknob
That said: "Please do not derange."

"Naughty man," she said,
"You have broken La Loi
So now you are under arrest!
You must come quietly," she told me
And then I did,
All over her dress

Louise, Louise
I'm down on my knees
At this game I am somewhat newish
Louise, Louise, do whatever you please
Beat me, whip me
Tell me I'm Jewish

"French must be protected
From English!" she said
As I was admiring her figure
Then I saw that she did have
Some cause for complaint
For I was at least one third bigger

She took out a tape measure
And gave me a look
And I must say it gave me a scare

Till I saw that she only
Intended to measure
The size of my dick ~ tionnaire

Louise, Louise
I'm begging you please
Let's get married without delay
And then we'll have children
And they'll be allowed
To go to school en Anglais!

Brave Sir Mordecai

The economy was in ruins
The premier wore a frown
"We've no jobs," the people cried
"And the stadium's falling down!
Will no one soothe our fevered brows?
Will no one even try?"
"I will do my best," replied
Brave Sir Mordecai

And off he rode, this dauntless knight
To far off New York City
To say, in reams of matchless prose
That things at home were shitty

This article left nothing out
It covered every angle
Of the Franco-Anglo 400-Year-Old
Linguistic wrangle

The tone of it was factual
It was fair and not too shrewish
Honest and unflinching
(And only slightly Jewish)

Sir Peladeau was heard to say
A sneer upon his face
"I do not like Sir Mordecai
He takes up too much space!"
"I do not like the things he said
Nor the way he said it."
Quoth Mordecai: "I know not why
I'm sure he has not read it."

And bravely he stood by his work
A lonely shining star
"Things are not perfect here," he said
"I will not say they are
So let them bay and let them rant
I for one will not recant
They can say the earth is flat
I know it's not. And that is that."

And sure enough the raging mob
Retreated from their prey
Sir Parizeau he merely sniffed
"'Twas boring, anyway

He doesn't understand our habits
He should stick to Duddy Kravitz
He doesn't seem to comprehend
He needs my boot in his rear end."

Six months have passed
Not much has changed
On our part of the planet
Sir Mordecai has put out a book
Someone wants to ban it

You'd think it was an earthquake
Not just a little tale
It scored at least a ten
On the Richler scale

"But with all the fuss and bother
In the Quebec nation
I rather doubt," said Mordecai
"There'll be a French translation

Their ancestors were prostitutes
I researched it with precision
It could have been much worse
At least they weren't politicians

Oh Canada, Oh Quebec
I know not which the worse is
But you know I feel sometimes
Like I wrote The Satanic Verses"

But brave Sir Mordecai, he felt
That he had done his task
"The people bade me help them
And I did what they asked."

And off he rode, back to his home
In the townships of Quebec
A giant of a writer
And a real pain in the neck

It's Good To Be A Goy In Montreal

Rick: *What is a goy?*

George: *A goy is someone who thinks a yarmulke is a motorcycle.*
A goy is someone who thinks Yom Kippur means that fish over there.
A goy is someone who thinks Hebrew is the third person singular of the verb: to brew.
A goy is someone who, when he hears the word putz, thinks of golf.

Rick: *So a goy is - us?*

George: *Yes. Goys R us.*

I felt lost and alone
In a sea of Francophones
I was looking for a way to finagle
A way to stick around
In this ever-changing town
My lifesaver turned out to be a bagel
I no longer wanted to rent a moving truck
I no longer felt
As if I was a schmuck
We can stay together
If we function as a group
What this country needs
Is a bowl of chicken soup

It won't help
It couldn't hurt!

Oy! Oy! Oy! There's so much to enjoy
Come to where the portions are not small
Oy! Oy! Oy! Every girl and boy
It's good to be a goy in Montreal!

Traditions today
Are waning away
But to me they're not just ephemeral
So when my son arrived
To have him circumcised
I had to take him to Jewish General
Until then, I was the sort of man

Who thought the "Jewish General"
Was Moshe Dayan
A question of etiquette
Into my mind did slip
When your son is circumcised
Do you leave a tip?

Oy! Oy! Oy! There's so much to enjoy
You don't have to be a Sadie or a Sol
Oy! Oy! Oy! Every girl and boy
It's good to be a goy in Montreal!

I like to take my belly
Into a Jewish deli
And eat a little smoked meat on rye bread
One thing bothers me
How can you be
Kosher and be living in Ham – stead?
Some Jewish delis ran afoul of the law
Sol's Bagel Basement isn't called that anymore
The name has been changed
And if you give them a call
They'll answer the phone
"Hello, Bagel Sous Sol!"

Oy! Oy! Oy! There's so much to enjoy
Come to where the portions are not small
Oy! Oy! Oy! Every girl and boy
It's good to be a goy in Montreal!

St. Patrick's Day Parade

At the time we wrote "Everybody's Irish On St. Patrick's Day" there had been a big controversy about gays and lesbians marching in the Boston parade. Because of it they cancelled their parade that year, and Montreal's became the longest continually running St. Patrick's parade in North America by default.

To celebrate, we finished our song with a triumphant: "Whether you're heterosexual, bisexual or gay," there was a pause with a rising arpeggio for effect, and then: "Everybody's Irish On St. Patrick's Day!"

Then we sang along with our own recording, all along the parade route. The sound-man started it up again as we approached the reviewing stand at Phillips Square.

As Murphy's Law would have it, our float stopped just before University Street. And as the song inexorably progressed I began to realize with horror which line we were destined to be singing as we passed.

Sure enough, when we finally lurched in front of the Mayor, The Archbishop and the Parade Marshall, we were singing the final crescendo of our song. The words: "Whether you are heterosexual, bisexual, or gay," rang out loud and clear. And the word "gay" was followed by the musical pause, just as our float stopped dead.

For what seemed like an eternity the word bounced off The Bay and Birk's, the jewellers. "Gay! Gay!" and off all the buildings around Phillips Square, "Gay! Gay!" as we looked at the dignitaries and they looked back at us.

Their mouths hung open in disbelief.

And then finally the line "Everybody's Irish On St. Patrick's Day" ended their suspense and we lurched on down St. Catherine Street and out of their sight.

Everybody's Irish On St. Patrick's Day

Everybody's smiling
As they march in the parade
There's something that they're drinking
And it isn't lemonade
Whether you are black or white
Or even old and grey
Everybody's Irish on St. Patrick's Day

It's a festival to celebrate
The coming of the spring
And even if it's freezing
You can't feel a thing
There's a million Irish bodies
To keep the cold away
Everybody's Irish on St. Patrick's Day

In the middle of the road
There's a line of green paint
The parade Marshall's standing there
Looking kinda quaint
And everyone can sing
And dance about without restraint
And all because St. Patrick was a saint
And we ain't

We'll have some Irish whiskey
And we'll eat some Irish grub
And we'll have an Irish sing-along
In an Irish pub
And Irish eyes are smiling
To carry us away
Everybody's Irish on St. Patrick's Day

Each St. Patrick's Sunday
We try to begin
With a traditional Irish breakfast
Of a beer and a poutine
Whether you're heterosexual
Bisexual or gay
Everybody's Irish on St. Patrick's Day

The Night They Invented Poutine

The night they invented poutine
It was a most peculiar scene
Ginette Reno was shy and thin
The Nordiques began to win
Jacques Parizeau sang
"God Save the Queen!"
The night they invented poutine

No one knows the precise origin
Where or when this food did begin
Everybody in Quebec
Will tell you with a grin
It was their little village
That invented the poutine

FREE TRADE

To be really authentic
The potatoes must be old
The gravy must be hot
And the cheese must be cold
With a Journal de Montréal
Wherever it is sold
And served with a roll
In a bowl by a troll

You put some potatoes
And some cheese in a tin
But the cheese won't melt
Till you put the gravy in
Then it sticks to your fork
And dribbles down your chin
And that's how you know
That you're eating a poutine

If the French fries are greasy
And the gravy's nice and hot
The cheese curds melt
As they come out of the pot
But once in your stomach

They congeal into a knot
If your food does that
Then poutine is what you've got

Some use mozzarella
But that isn't really it
And they serve it at McDonald's
But the French fries are shit
And I hate to be picky
But I have to admit
It's hard to eat
When the cook
Has a zit!

There's no way anyone
Would call it haute cuisine
But it isn't really junk food
It's something in between
But it's better than a burger
Or a Mike's submarine
A balanced diet
Is a beer and a poutine!

C'est La Faute Du Fédéral

The people of Quebec
Are having a lot of stress
Even Gilles Vigneault
Has changed his name to
Gilles Vin-yes

I called Corrections Canada
They could not live up to their name
I cannot solve the problem
But I know who is to blame

When your voiture will not start
    C'est la faute du fédéral
When you have a broken heart
    C'est la faute du fédéral
Ce n'est jamais la faute du
Gouvernement provincial
Ni du municipal
    C'est la faute du fédéral

If you put on too much weight
    C'est la faute du fédéral
If you have a large prostate
    C'est la faute du fédéral
Si vous n'avez pas l'argent
Pour une vacance tropicale

Et faut rester à Montréal!
    C'est la faute du fédéral

C'est la faute du fédéral
C'est eux autres qui font le mal
Bienvenue au carnival
C'est la faute du fédéral

Violence on TV?
    C'est la faute du fédéral
If you are fed up with me
    C'est la faute du fédéral
Si vous avez l'impression
qu' la vie ne soit pas idéale
And they closed your hôpital
    C'est la faute du fédéral

La fuite du capitale
    C'est la faute du fédéral
La merde du cheval
    C'est la faute du fédéral
Le déclin inexorable
Du Canadien de Montreal
C'est pas ma faute
    C'est la faute du fédéral
    Excusez, la!

In March 1996 Lucien Bouchard made a speech at the Centaur Theatre in Montreal to reassure the province's Anglophones of their future under his Parti Québécois government.

Lucien Bouchard's Centaur Speech

I am here to build a bridge to the Anglophone community of Quebec. Like all bridges it will be beautiful, it will be strong, it will be constantly in need of repair; and on weekends it will be closed, for no reason at all.

My topic tonight is: Living together before, during, and after the referendum. Which, in Quebec, is all of the time.

There will be another referendum. And next time the question will be clear. I have the text of this question: "Are you sure you don't want to not separate, yes or no?"

Quebecers want to live in a country of our own. Jacques Parizeau has already begun to live in a world of his own.

M. Parizeau is, for me, too "hard line." I hear that he has a map of Canada tattooed on his rear end. When he bends down, Quebec separates.

I believe that it is possible to have linguistic peace here in Quebec. Linguistic peace is like underwear. Sometimes it just creeps up on you.

I am concerned about partition. More concerned even than was René Lévesque. His partition was here (pointing to one ear) and went all the way over to here (pointing to other ear).

It saddens me to hear that the best and brightest of Quebec's Anglophones have left. But, you are still here!

George: *It is so unfair. When they have referendums they always make us federalists be on the "No" side. So when we put up a sign that says: "No" Rally Tonight, nobody goes.*

The Referendum Tango

It's the referendum tango
The choice between "Yes" and "No"
Maybe you can run but you can't hide
You can flip and you can flop
But when the flipping has to stop
You simply can't decide to un-decide

We're floating on an ocean
Of Francophone emotion
Our breasts all heave, our eyes are wet
To a rhythm that is Latin
The swish of silk and satin
As Lucien waves his big magic baguette

Dance the referendum tango
They're wearing blue
They're wearing red
Dance the referendum tango
They will mislead
We'll be misled
It's another crisis of October
And it won't even be over
When it's over!

They call it democratic
A simple mathematic
But actually we know that it's not
And if you don't believe that's true
Then I've got two words for you
Lobster pot

It's déjà vu all over again
It wasn't that long ago when
We danced like this until we were a wreck
And if you wonder why it's so
I guess it's just 'cause "No means no"
Everywhere – Except Quebec

Dance the referendum tango
They're wearing blue
They're wearing red
Dance the referendum tango
They will mislead
We'll be misled
It's another crisis of October
And it won't even be over
When it's over!

Rick: *How about Parizeau's speech the morning after?*
Monique Simard tried to explain. "Hey, he's resigning," she said.
"What more do you want, a public stoning?" No, I thought.
Being publicly stoned was what got him into trouble in the first place.

Money And The Ethnic Vote

Money and the ethnic vote
Money and the ethnic vote
It ended on a sour note
Money and the ethnic vote

It's amazing how one's fortunes
So suddenly can turn
On Halloween our premier
Became a Jacques-o-lantern

When he went to Bermuda
To sun tan his pot belly
We ethnics got our revenge
We sent his luggage to Delhi!

Money and the ethnic vote
Money and the ethnic vote
It's always the same scapegoat
Money and the ethnic vote!

Great Canadian Disasters

There's a Canadian tradition
To sing a rugged song
Accentuating all the things
That go completely wrong

The Edmund Fitzgerald
Went down with all hands aboard
Gordon Lightfoot sang about it
And won a Juno award

We sing of brave explorers
Where they've gone to no one knows
How they travelled to the Arctic
And everybody froze

Saint Jean de Brébeuf
Will always be remembered
He was captured by the Iroquois
And gradually dismembered

But you'll never hear us sing about
Roberta Bondar's flight
We minstrels aren't inspired
When everything goes right

We love to drink so deeply
From life's bitter cup
There's nothing like disaster
To cheer Canadians up

The mysterious disappearance of Sir John Franklin finally explained...

Oh, Alberta!

Sung by Preston Manning

On election night
It was quite a sight
There on the TV screen
Quebec was distinct
Ontario was pink
But out west the map turned green

No more wishin'
I'm leader of the opposition
Now it's finally come to pass
If you don't agree
You can take your fleur de lys
And stick it up your national ass-embly

Oh, Alberta
I'm another feller
They discovered at Drumheller
Oh, Alberta
Home of the dinosaur

We've got a great new look
We've balanced our books
Thanks to a wonderful guy named Ralph
Yes, we're conservative out here
Our women wear brassieres
Hell, I'm even wearing one myself

Those easterners
With their masseurs and their liqueurs
Think I'm a chump and a frump
I'll get 'em in a herd
And then, one word
Head-Smashed-In-Buffalo-Jump

Oh, Alberta
Your winds made me warm
When you voted for Reform
Oh, Alberta
Home of the dinosaur

Sympathy For The Indian

George: *Canadian Indians would prefer self-government. Columbus showed them what ours would be like. When he left, he didn't know where he was going. When he got there, he didn't know where he was. When he returned, he didn't know where he had been. All he achieved was to screw everything up for the locals. And he did it all with other people's money.*

I'm Ovide Mercredi
People get ready
(At the national assembly everybody blinked)
I got my feathers and my drums
And my ancient tribal hums
(You want distinct? We'll show you distinct!)
We can fix the constitution
With a big powwow
(As the Indian said to the mermaid: "How?")

Vote for me
And I'll set you free
(Your understanding of history
Will be a lot deeper)
You'll be leaner and meaner
The land will be cleaner
(And your cigarettes
Will be a whole lot cheaper)
We are the people of the midnight sun
(How come he gets thirty feathers
And I only get one?)

Pleased to meet you
Hope you're doing fine
But that land you're living on
Is really mine
I'm chief and this headdress
Makes it legal
(Somewhere in the world there's a bald eagle)

It's not just for me
It's about the Cree
(I think by now
We've all heard their version)
Hydro Quebec
Shows too little respect
(Something to do with total immersion!)
How can they do that to us
The First Nations?
(We should've had a policy on immigration)

When the Mohawks were in court
They had a lot of support
(People taking time off from hugging trees)
Lasagne got a sentence
That was too intense
(30 minutes at 400 degrees)
They say we ought to speak French
But we're not gonna do it
(It was hard enough to learn Inuit)

Pleased to meet you
Hope you're doing fine
But that land you're living on
Is really mine
I am the messenger the Indians sent
(To collect 350 years back rent)

I'm Not The Kind Of Guy

George: *Merci, du fonds de mon coeur.*
Thank you, from the heart of my bottom.

Rick: *Oh, you speak French.*

George: *Yes. I'm not the kind of guy who thinks
a coup de grace is a lawnmower.*

Rick: *Vous parlez francais.*

George: *Yes. I'm not the kind of guy who thinks a cul de sac
is a vasectomy, or that bon appetit means small penis.*

Rick: *You're bilingual.*

George: *Certainement. I'm not the kind of guy who thinks that an
aperitif is a set of dentures, or that a pas de deux is a father of twins.*

Rick: *You speak the language of Molière.*

George: *Yes. I'm not the kind of guy who thinks Jeanne-d'Arc means
there's no light in the washroom, or that au contraire is a deodorant.
And I'm certainly not the kind of guy who thinks douane is the name of
the guy who works for Canada customs.*

George: *In Montreal, in the summer, there are lots of festivals. It all starts in June, with the Grand Prix. As far as Quebec is concerned, it's 'F' 1 in June and 'F' you' the rest of the year.*

Driving In Quebec

*In Quebec there's no right turn on red
Too many people would end up dead
At every corner they need a cop
Never mind turn on red
They don't even stop*

*They drive like they're trying
To break the record
The Quebec flag ought to be checkered
Montreal is like the Monte Carlo rally
They even had to put speed bumps
In the alley*

*Red light, green light – what the heck
We love driving in Quebec
From Chicoutimi to Maine
It's – beep beep
Get outa my lane*

*This is the only place I've ever seen
Where they have to put up a sign that says
"Wait for the green"
No matter how late you cross on yellow
Up your rear end is some other fellow*

*Pedestrians have only one light
It doesn't say "Walk"
It says: "Run for your life!"
How far is it across Boulevard Lévesque?
No one knows – no one's ever made it yet*

*Red light, green light – what the heck
We love driving in Quebec
From Chicoutimi to Maine
It's – beep beep
Get outa my lane
It's – beep beep
The drivers are mad 'cause the
Beep beeping roads
Are so bad*

The Gunshine State

I like to go away
On a Florida holiday
Where the guns shine in the sunshine
In "The Gunshine State"

The muggers salivate
When they see my rental plates
Where the guns shine in the sunshine
In "The Gunshine State"

They can tell that we're Canadians
From the things we say
I don't know how they do it
Like, it's amazing, eh?
They mug us 'cause they know that
We will never go to court
Or come back to Florida without a police escort

We don't carry guns because
We know people get hurt
Bearing arms in Canada means
Taking off your shirt
Our idea of violence is usually no more
Than trying to seat five people
At a table meant for four

I'm afraid my sunscreen
Won't stop an M-16
Where the guns shine in the sunshine
In "The Gunshine State"

They know where I'm from
When I put my Speedo on
Where the guns shine in the sunshine
In "The Gunshine State"

A lifeguard keeps us covered
Sunbathing at the shore
A bodyguard keeps us covered
Going to the convenience store
Feel the excitement from Key West
To Jacksonville
If a hurricane don't get us
A mugger probably will

Next season local papers
Won't make fun of us
Like they did quite recently
That caused so much fuss
'Cause this time when I'm photographed
I will look my best
My big bedaine hidden
Behind a bulletproof vest!

Insurance that is best
Covers combat stress
Where the guns shine in the sunshine
In "The Gunshine State"

I'll be quite the charmer
In my body armour
Where the guns shine in the sunshine
In "The Gunshine State"

I Live In Westmount

I live in Westmount
And I'm glad that I do
Live in Westmount
You'd be very glad too

The joy of Westmount is complete
At the corner of Victoria and Sherbrooke street
There's everything that Westmount stands for
Three banks and a liquor store!

I live in Westmount
And I'm proud to be
In lower Westmount
Or Upper Saint-Henri

Here I sit in the Westmount sun
To the sound of an Italian mowing my lawn
Living in Westmount is perfect bliss
I can pretend Quebec doesn't exist

Westmount – such a lovely place
With golden agers dressed in white
With smiles on their face
Westmount – it's the place for me
With kids in uniforms going to schools
That charge outrageous fees

I live in Westmount
And I'm glad that I do
Live in Westmount
And now Mulroney does, too

Two terms as P.M. and times are hard
Brian's slipped below the Boulevard
He must be glad he didn't go for three
He might have ended up in NDG
I live in Westmount

Things you'll never hear in Westmount

May I borrow your copy of La Presse?

Dad, I'd like to work this summer.

How about those Leafs, eh?

I bought this at the thrift store.

Have another glass of Harfeng de Neiges.

Aren't trailer parks wonderful!

That's a nice beret.

Salut gaston!

Rick: *Here we are in the Townships, where bumper stickers say: "If it's tourist season, why can't I shoot one?"*

George: *They've got all kinds of ethical dilemmas in the Townships. Like, if two Townshippers get divorced, are they still cousins?*

We Are Townshippers

We are Townshippers
Not Cantonneurs de l'est
We are Townshippers
The Townships are the best
We are Townshippers
And we are proud to be
It's a good, good life in the Townships

Down here the ducks
Are held in high regard
A whole lot of people
Work for canard
(I work hard, too!)
We breed 'em, we raise 'em
We trade 'em and we truck 'em
We feed 'em and we fatten 'em
And finally we
Pluck 'em

We are Townshippers
We do things our own way
We are Townshippers
We vote for Jean Charest
We are Townshippers
Come roll in the hay
It's a good, good life in the Townships

There was a farmer near the borderline
Who won a million on the 6-49
What will he do with the money that he won?
I guess he'll keep farming until it's all gone

We are Townshippers
Drivin' our combines
We are Townshippers
We put up English signs
We are Townshippers
But we will not be cowed
It's a good, good life in the Townships

Sugar shack, cow plop
Barn wood, chicken plucker
Corn cob, dirt road
Antique store
She was only a farmer's daughter
Ah, but all the horse men knew 'er
(I knew 'er, too!)

We are Townshippers
Our dairy farms are great
We are Townshippers
Our milk won't separate
We are Townshippers
And we're not shipping out
It's a good, good life
In the Townships

Things Your Wife Will Never Say

You have all the bed covers, I'll be fine.

Every time you tell that joke, it gets better.

That beer belly makes you look distinguished.

Omigod, we're running out of duct tape.

Get a whiff of that one!

Don't get up.

My parents are coming over tonight,
why don't you go out drinking with your buddies?

My goodness, what a beautiful scrotum.

Flick through all the TV channels again, it's so soothing.

I'm sorry, you're right.

Rick: *And now ladies and gentlemen, introducing the leader of her majesty's opposition, M. Lucien Bouchard, known to his close friends as Lulu. You might say "Lulu's back in town."*

Dancing With Lulu

Jackie: I'm dancing with Lulu
He dances so well
But Lulu's not happy with me
I can tell
We're dancing together
From mutual need
We both want to dance
But we both want to lead

Softly, so softly
I hear Lulu groan
I fear Lulu'd rather
Be dancing alone
He sighs and his eyes
Grow misty, and then –
Perhaps Lulu's thinking of Brian again

Dancing with Lulu
This moment should be divine
I'm dancing with Lulu
But Lulu will never be mine

Pour le peuple, pour le peuple
Pour le peuple Québécois
Le peuple Québécois
Le peuple Québécois
Pour le peuple, pour le peuple
Pour le peuple Québécois
C'est maintenant la prochaine fois

Lulu: You may be surprised
To see me this way
It's something new
That I'm trying today
I will wear a dress
And make no objection
If it will help Jackie
Achieve an election

Next time I go
To the U.S. of A.
I'm going to make certain
That I'm dressed this way

Since J. Edgar Hoover
I hear they're impressed
By a middle-aged man
Who is wearing a dress

Dancing with Lulu
It's the 24th of June
I'm dancing with Lulu
Listen, they're playing our tune

Waving flags
Speaking French
Marching out in the street
With our fists in the air
We don't have a care

Waving flags
Speaking French
Life is complete
And I'm dancing with Lulu again

Jackie: For God's sake Lulu – get in step.
Lulu: I would Jackie, but you are dancing on my feet.
Jackie: You have such big feet, by jove.
Lulu: How would you know? You have never seen your feet.

The big question for Canadians is:
Is space a federal or a provincial jurisdiction?

Canadians In Space

Ten (dix) nine (neuf) eight (huit) seven (sept)
Six (six) five (cinq) four (quatre) three (trois)
Two (deux) one (un)
Blast off! (tabernac!)

Canadians are astronauts
Well, who ever would have thought
Not just in insurance or in banks
From Cape Kennedy to space
Back to Edwards Air Force Base
Now it's Marc Garneau and not Tom Hanks

Canadians are not impressed
By how the astronauts are dressed
The sealed suit a spacewalk does require
In winter we all dress that way
So when we see them what we say
Is "You can buy those at Canadian Tire"

Oo – I'm a spaceman
Way up in the outer atmosphere
Oo – I'm a spaceman
I think I can see my house from here

It's only natural I thought
For us to be an astronaut
If that's what we really want to do
Ready now to take our place
Way out there in outer space
We'll see things from
Preston Manning's point of view!

95

The Only Straight Waiter In The Bloor Street Diner

There's a diner near Yorkville
Down on Bloor street
Where Toronto night people all go to eat
The food's nothing special
The service is slow
But at two in the morning
Where else can you go?

She said: "That waiter
Is the catch of the day
But ain't it a shame
He's probably gay."
Our server overheard 'er
And he put down a plate
He said: "Listen, sweetheart
Let's get one thing straight!

My moustache is trimmed
And my clothes are designer
But I'm the only straight waiter
In the Bloor Street Diner"

His pants were so tight
That you could tell
Not only his gender
But his religion as well
As he gave the table
A couple of wipes
He said: "Don't get hung up
On stereotypes

I know how to cook
And I know how to cry
I'm a modern, sensitive
New age guy
But there's no gay lover
At home in my flat
Not that there's anything wrong with that

My moustache is trimmed
And my clothes are designer
But I'm the only straight waiter
In the Bloor street diner"

They married last summer
Though I didn't go
And moved into a townhouse
In Etobicoke
With a mortgage, a minivan
A kid and a some pets
And that's just about as straight as it gets

Yes she married the man
Whose clothes were designer
The only straight waiter
In the Bloor street diner

Rick: I was playing a round of golf with some friends when a funeral cortege went by. I took off my hat and bowed my head as the procession passed.

George: Wow. That shows great respect.

Rick: Yeah. It was the least I could do.

After all, we'd been married for over thirty years.

Let's Play Golf

Golf! Slip the starter a fin
Golf! So that we can begin
Golf! Hey, let's play golf

Golf is wonderful
Who could scoff?
At getting up at the crack of dawn
On my day off
And later on when evening falls
I admire the sunset as I wash my balls

My short game
Works well for me
The only problem is
It's off the tee
By the time I reach the eighteenth green
I've been in places
The Indians haven't seen

Golf! I'm yelling "Fore!"
Golf! But eight is my score
Golf! Hey, let's play golf

When it comes to golf
I never scrimp
When else can a middle-aged man
Dress like a pimp?
And golf must be the only sport where
I can spend the whole day with hookers
And my wife doesn't care

The other day I played
With my friend Fred
And on the seventh hole
Fred dropped dead
It was the worst day I ever had
The memory of it still makes me sad

Hit the ball - drag Fred
Hit the ball - drag Fred
Golf! Hey let's play golf

Golf! But I'm not complaining
Golf! Unless it's raining
Golf! Hey let's play golf

Tough Crowd

We're a tough crowd, we're Canadian
In business we're not slack
Our country has produced
Tycoons like Conrad Black
I'm a bit like Conrad
I can truly say
I got up and bought a newspaper today

We're tough, we're tough
We're very, very tough

We're a tough crowd, we're Canadian
Our snowboarders excel
They are sponsored by "Roots"
And seeds and stems, as well
We've got world-class comedians
Who get paid enormous fees
I don't mean Jim Carrey –
I mean our MPs

We're a tough crowd, we're Canadian
As tough as leather boots
We send our armies into wars
And tell them not to shoot
The Canadian soldier
Is the toughest in the world
k.d. Lang is the army's pin-up girl

We're tough, we're tough
We're very, very tough

I Don't Want To Hear About Clinton's Thing

I don't want to hear about Clinton's thing
And he doesn't care about mine
If I never hear about it again
Far as I'm concerned that'll be fine
If he smothers himself in cold Jell-O
And bangs all his secretaries
One at a time
It's a story as old as the Capitol hills
But it's not a capital crime

I don't really care about Clinton's thing
Or his other acts of Congress
I don't really care how he gets his kicks
Or what's on Monica's dress
I don't really care if it's bodily fluids
Or porridge or soup or lychee
And I couldn't say if it's
DNA, TSP, MSG or PP

I don't really care about Clinton's thing
Or the details of his private life
But I have the greatest respect for the woman
Who's stuck with being his wife
She keeps her dignity, stays on her toes

While the blows fall thick and fast
It must be difficult being first lady
When you know you aren't the last

I don't really care about Clinton's thing
Or its physical attributes
If it's bent or it's straight or it's so bloody long
That he keeps one end stuck in his boot
When he went on TV it occurred to me
That he really shouldn't have tried
He just should have taken his pecker out
And said: "There! I hope you're satisfied!"

I don't really care about Clinton's thing
I'd much rather talk about mine
Frankly it's starting to make me sick
That they talk about his all the time
I'm not even envious, I'm OK
And if he's having fun well that's fine
But I don't want to hear about his anymore
I'd much rather talk about
Hear about, sing about
Much rather talk about mine

Things Your Husband Will Never Say

There's something
different about you,
I noticed it right away.

No thanks,
Sometimes I just like
to be held.

I'll have a white wine
spritzer please.

Gee – I never knew
looking at colour swatches
could be so interesting.

Tell our dinner guests about
when you gave birth.

Hey – let's rent
"Bridges of Madison County"
again.

She's cute but I find
her boobs are too big.

I'm depressed – let's go
shopping!

Talk to me.

You drive,
you're better at it.

♩♩...AND ALL THAT JAZZ!

I'll Always Think Of You

They say nostalgia
Ain't what it used to be
But that's not true for me
Because I long for
Those times when we were free
And we could say: "Hello"
In the town I used to know

I'll always think of you
With everything I do
The way you used to be
Now that it's history

A faded photograph
Evokes a bitter laugh
Sometimes it seems a shame
That things don't stay the same

The old man who
Is pointing to
A space up in mid-air
Says: "See that spot
Above that lot
I used to live right there"

I'll always think of you
The town I somehow knew
I see it everywhere
As though it was still there

The way the world was then
Seems like a heaven
And when I'm gone you know
That's where I hope to go

These CDs are available from our web site.

Live

Troubadours

Humour for Boomers

ACKNOWLEDGEMENTS

Many of the tracks on the accompanying CD were performed in front of
live Canadians and recorded for CBC Radio's "Madly Off in All Directions"
all across Canada: Charlottetown, St. John's, Quebec City, Winnipeg, and Edmonton.
We would like to thank Lorne Elliott, Françoise Doliveux, Bryan Hill, and Ray Folcik
for this opportunity. Other tracks on the CD were produced for CBC Radio in
Montreal, Quebec, by the indefrankatigable Frank Opolko.

We would also like to thank the Centaur Theatre Company of Montreal
for their support, and musical-comedy director Corey Castle for his perceptive guidance.
Many of these songs found their genesis there.

Thanks also to Andy Nulman and Bruce Hills of "Just for Laughs"
for their friendship and their faith in our work.
Many of these songs were performed at their world famous comedy festival.

Thanks to the Pipes and drums of the Black Watch, Royal Highland Regiment of Canada
for their contribution to "'Twas The Scots That Built This Country."

Thanks also to Duke Braun, sound technician to the gods.
Thanks to Terry Mosher, Mary Hughson,
and Kim McArthur for making this book possible.

To find out more about Bowser and Blue concerts and recordings,
please visit our web site at

bowserandblue.com

PHOTO CREDITS:
Cover and page 7; George Belinsky;
Pages 1, 5, 11, 68, 104, 105; John Sleeman;
Pages 58, 93; Lewis Blau

Aislin is the name of Terry Mosher's elder daughter and the *nom de plume* he uses as the editorial page cartoonist for *The Gazette* in Montreal. Mosher is also the cartoon editor of *Maclean's*, Canada's national magazine. The recipient of many awards, in May of 2003 Terry Mosher was invested as an Officer of the Order of Canada.

Mosher has produced thirty-five books including numerous collections of his own Aislin cartoons and other works that he has illustrated. His latest collection entitiled *In Your Face* was published in the fall of 2001 and is available from *McArthur & Company* along with many other recent books by Aislin.

For more information, visit

www.aislin.com

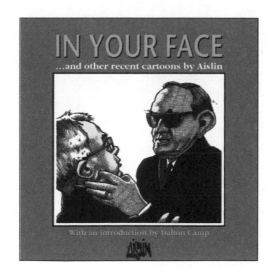